INDIOS

INDIOS

A poem . . .
a performance

Linda Hogan

with a Preface by the author
and a Foreword by
Lois Beardslee, Ph.D.

San Antonio, Texas
2012

Indios © 2012 by Linda Hogan
Cover image and frontispiece: Digital drawing by Dustin Mater

First Edition

Print Edition ISBN: 978-0-916727-85-7
ePub ISBN: 978-1-60940-165-8
Kindle ISBN: 978-1-60940-166-5
PDF ISBN: 978-1-60940-167-2

Wings Press
627 E. Guenther
San Antonio, Texas 78210
Phone/fax: (210) 271-7805

On-line catalogue and ordering:
www.wingspress.com
All Wings Press titles are distributed to the trade by
Independent Publishers Group • www.ipgbook.com

Library of Congress Cataloging-in-Publication Data:

Hogan, Linda.
  Indios : a poem ... a performance / Linda Hogan ; with an intro-
duction by Lois Beardslee, Ph.D. -- 1st ed.
     p. cm.
  ISBN 978-0-916727-85-7 (hardback, printed edition : alk. pa-
per) -- ISBN 978-1-60940-165-8 (epub ebook) -- ISBN 978-
1-60940-166-5 (kindle ebook) -- ISBN 978-1-60940-167-2
(library pdf ebook)
  I. Title.
  PS3558.O34726I53 2012
  811'.54--dc23   2011026507

Contents

This book is dedicated to all indigenous women of the world who know this story from our histories.

It is dedicated to my daughters, granddaughters, and my great-granddaughter, Jayla. It is for Tanya, Vivian, Cammie, Danielle, my two Michaels, Angel, and Jasmine.

It is also for my brother, Larry, and sisters, Donna and Anna.

For David and your support.

And to the trees, earth, waters, and life forms all around us. Thank you.

Foreword

Linda Hogan's poetry and fiction alike share a certain shape-shifting ability that elevates daily events to events of significance. Hogan entices readers with the ordinary, pulling us into worlds so accurately drawn that we feel comfortable with the sheer familiarity of the flora and fauna, the landscapes, the human situations. It begins so simply, so safely—safe in the sense that the reader believes that one will *not* find oneself lost deep in emotional woods or struck by lightning-like revelations.

And yet Linda Hogan's work has a way of gradually changing simplicity into complexity, pain into beauty, the mundane into the sacred. She makes one cringe with the sound of a snapping bone, makes the reader quake and pull back, and then makes that same reader fall in love with that painful event only a few lines or paragraphs later. Such manifestations of intellect, insight and emotion reside on the razor's edge of human vulnerability, and Hogan knows when and how to push readers over the edge with directional control.

Although much of the poem *Indios* is drawn from experiences that have, over time, become heavily romanticized, this work is rooted in reality and sincerity. Hogan's is an authority drawn from spirit and blood and land. Her Indios is a woman who speaks for generations of indigenous women, transcending time and space. Indios is a Native woman falsely incarcerated for the inadvertent deaths of her children. This tragedy resulted from her persistent efforts to save her children. The situation was beyond her control. Her options were limited. But Indios is beyond being merely a victim; she is the ur-Indian mother, the ultimate symbol of love and dedication to the future; and her story starts with intercontinental contact, the arrival of the first Europeans in the "new" world.

A "performance poem" developed for a single voice, we realize as Indios relates her own story that the character acts as an echo chamber for aboriginal women throughout history. The reader has no choice but to hear in Indios echoes of Malinche, wife of Cortez, simultaneously blessed as the mother of *mestizos* and cursed as a traitor to her people. Likewise we hear echoes of Pocahontas, of La Llorona, and ultimately, of Medea—not, Hogan stresses, the Medea of Euripides' play, but the captured princess of the original story in which her children were murdered by the people of Corinth and Medea herself was feared and despised for her cultural differences and knowledge. Hogan's Indios refers to herself as an "aftershock" of history, a term that many contemporary Native Americans would embrace.

Indios speaks to an interviewer whom we neither see nor hear. She warns the interviewer, and thus us, not to love her, not to sympathize with her too much, nor to believe in her innocence. Hogan makes little easy for her audience by offering up a complex character whom we can love only for the tragedy of her circumstances, not for her actions. But this is not romanticized history. It is a world pared down to the very basics of human nature and circumstance.

It is important that *Indios* is not only a poem, but a performance. A reader can see Indios glide across her cell or brush back her hair with a tired hand. It is no hard task to imagine her face inside of harsh walls, to hear her speak to you and only you, directly to your soul. It is also possible to see her memories, to imagine her fleeing on horseback or on a sun-drenched and sandy beach, a young and beautiful girl welcoming the first Europeans with wide and innocent eyes, unaware they are there for the taking of trees, land, children, history, culture, identity. This work is a melding of tangible experience. The character and the words take on lives of their own in the imagination and vision that each reader brings to the page. *Indios* offers revelations of our grandmothers and great, great grandmothers on Indian land. As a Native reader, I feel Indios has spoken on my behalf; I feel less alone.

Linda Hogan ranks among the most vocal and ground-breaking of Native American authors, successfully reaching into the hearts and minds of readers of all cultural backgrounds and finding commonalities. With this particular story Hogan has done something seemingly impossible: she speaks of undressing "a five hundred year old wound," and she accomplishes this by breathing beauty into the damaged flesh and soul. That open wound, one that denies Indios her own land, her own story, becomes accessible to all readers in words that begin with organic simplicity and rise to the task of acknowledging history and contemporary class structure. Ultimately, the story of Indios is about how to salvage the future.

With *Indios* Hogan has become a force gently pushing continents into psychological cooperation for future generations, creating a transformational work that stretches for centuries in a language that does not know time. Reading *Indios*, I hear and become the woman Indios; I feel that I am among countless women who are joining Hogan and her protagonist shouting, singing along with this woman who voices our sentiments while we intentionally make our way in and out of the centuries and worlds our mothers have given us. You'd better listen.

Lois Beardslee
Author of *Not Far Away*

Author's Preface

Many years ago when I first heard the story of the woman Medea, I recognized it as the same story as that of an Indian woman who married a white man of power. It is a story from many of our histories. It is beauty married to tragedy and is common to all continents.

We aboriginal people know this story well. As Buffy St. Marie, one of our great musicians, says, "I knew America when I was just a girl."

As for me, I knew Medea when *she* was just a girl.

When I researched the story, I found that originally her children—not the ones of the later rendering of the Greek tragedy—had been stoned by those who feared a mixed-blood child would come to power in their land. But the story of that time was changed for the sake of politics so that in the Greek tragedy *Medea,* the queen was recorded as the one who killed her children.

Our lives, as aboriginals, are filled with this monologue. I have created it here as both a performance piece of a woman interviewed in prison and as a long poem, to be sung, spoken, read aloud or in silence, to be thought about or wept over.

It is set in the timelessness of our lives. When we say that we crossed over the Trail of Tears, we did. It is in our Native memory. Time is different in the cell structure of bodies created from and on this continent. Yet I welcome all people, all of whom come from some land, belong to a place, to a history not unlike this one. I welcome them to this story, like the world, with both its sorrows and its great beauties.

Chukmashki,
Thank you,
Linda Hogan

INDIOS

Game

What? Do I hear children? Playing a game?
No, they are singing. They are dancing.
They are saying magical words.
Oh he yay yay,
oh he yay
Hey ai Lina,
Hey ai Lina........

You're Miss Finley.
Yes, I am the one they call Indios.
You want me to call you Clare.
I like that word, Clare,
And what it means.
No, it's fine. I knew you would be late.
No one expects the guards
To go through their perfumed bag
Or examine their underwear
So they won't smuggle something in to me.

No, I don't look like you expected.
Life hasn't hardened me here.

Yes, thank you. I do like sweets.
Yes, they take them away to examine as well.
Everything goes through the hands of the guards.
Even we go through their hands
As if we are water.
But then we have flowed through the hands
Of others all our lives,
Through the hands of husbands and fathers,
Falling through the writing hands of judges.
Some have fallen through the hands of their lawyers
And even their friends.
Some flow through the hands of one another.
We are like the element water,
Always flowing back
To some ocean
Of another humanity.

I hope you are not one of the people
Who have come to prove my innocence.
No? You only want to talk about my story?
The newspapers were full of this story.
Surely you read them.
But still you come to me,
As if my words will change the clouds of history.

And so much time has passed.
Sometimes I forget Time.
It was not our invention.

But then, it has been so long
And my story, like everything, even myself,
Has fallen through that element,
Time, as if it is water.

What does it mean, my name, Indios?
I am a Native woman.
We were called that in the beginning
Because, as Columbus wrote,
We were beautiful, alive, and generous.
When we were seen the first time,
He said we were *In Dios*. Of God. *Dios*.
I think of that. We were beautiful.

I see you have written questions for me.
You want to know how we met.
It was so long ago.
He came to our world.
I was just a girl, still a girl.
But when I saw him he was like a god to me
And something inside me changed.
He was shining.
I thought my father must have conjured up
This vision of my husband
When I saw him the first time
As he stood there in all his finery, shining.
And the sun was behind him.

I was bewitched,
Although later they called me the witching one
When I found water for them with a willow twig,
Me, a young girl who diagnosed illness,
Fixed a broken leg,
Helped women's bellies grow with child
And then helped them give birth, their way, not ours.

Still, I was the one witched by love
Or some feeling that overcame me
So suddenly, so powerfully,
And I was just a girl.

I was always a happy girl
Inside the walls of our little house
Inside the walls of my skin.
Even though I never had a mother,
My father could do anything.
He could build a shelter.
Together we grew corn.
He saw illness in a person.
He was a beautiful man.
We lived with our own people in our own world
On the earth we came from.
This earth.

My father could sing,
And when he did, his buffalo robe on his back,
He sang a song that would bring the whole world to a stop.
They say when he was young his songs could shake
Mountains or bring water to the surface of earth.

Still, when I saw the shining man
My heart jumped.
I was only twelve and knew no better.
I was like one of the fish that jump from water
Not aware the birds are waiting
To swallow them.

He landed his large boat near our home
To talk with my father about trading away the trees.
I didn't hear the conversation, just watched.
My father said, No. We didn't need money.
Selling the trees would have been the same
As trading away our sisters.

At first I wasn't part of any plan.
All the while they discussed these things,
I was young and my heart already taken by this man.
It was only later I realized
How much my father disliked him.
My father said No
To everything he wanted.

But I looked at him
With different eyes from afar.
Too far.

I wanted to touch his hair,
Then his face.
When the golden man touched my hand to say Good-bye
Even my body deceived me with its feelings.

I was like one of the falcons on his arm,
My eyes covered over,
Me the child of a man
Who could see the future,
Could read a human and know what they are.
But the heart has a mind of its own.
It will do what logic will not.

He returned. Much time passed and the time finally came
When they talked about what was to come.
My father knew. He could see
The future was bleak for us,
That it was going to be a breaking time
And they would do as they wanted
With our world, more of them every moment arriving
To take what they wished.

Then one day when the shining man saw me,
He, the man, sat thinking

Either that I was beautiful
Or he devised another plan
To marry me for what he wanted.
I will never know the reasons
For his ways, or if I was ever loved,
But devising is what the devious do—
And he was one of those.

He kept coming back to see us,
To talk with my father
And then to walk or sit with me.

Love is an old story,
One of kings whose kingdoms fell
Because of love,
Or a beautiful woman,
A mysterious note, a death,
All for love.
And nearly all the women in this prison
Are here for love or its betrayal.
Many worlds have fallen
Just for love which changed to something else.

When he told my father
What was to come,
Despite my father's resistance,
He knew it would be best to bring our worlds together.

9

It was inevitable, but that was the way
Of the new world.
And my poor father knew it.

While he and that man
who wrestled with spirits spoke,
I must have had a change of soul.
I went down to the water and I wept.
I was on my knees and I was weeping
Because some part of me felt the future.
My body must have known it was a game
I didn't want, not this way,
But now I was part of it, without choice,
And then there was my heart
With its own wishes.

I was too young to know.
We were of such different worlds.
My father could make a circle on the earth
And stand inside it and sing
The clouds toward us.
He was a sorcerer, they said of him in the other world,
But powerless like all men against greater weapons.

He foresaw what would happen.
He called me to him and said,
I dreamed there was no stopping

The change of the world
Without the whole of us being killed.
It is inevitable.
We will all soon be killed, moved, or contained
For what they want.
I didn't believe him at first.
But he said for me there was a hope
That in this position I could do something for my people
And for a while I did.

He said, You, my daughter, are strong.
For a time you will help us all.
Then you must return.
You are a stolen one, too young to know,
But remember, never forget, you are going to a place
Where our people are already their slaves
And still speak our language.
They will need you to keep life right for them.
And one day you may need them as well.
We are helpless
Against their laws
That are not our laws, not natural laws,
Not the laws from within our country
Which is now no longer ours.

So a time came that I went away.
I want you to know this is not only my story.

It is never the story of just one woman.
It is the telling of many worlds, peoples, and lands.

As for me, I was never a woman.
I was a city. I was a country.
This ordinary woman you see before you.
I have more freedom in prison
Than when I was a country and still just a girl.
My hair. It's not well arranged.
My clothing not fit for a queen.
My hands are dry and not oiled with perfumes
And I am worn down with labor
But at least I am not a country.
I am no longer trade goods.

When he took me home
Some said, How could you take such a wife?
I was a beauty then, and his younger brothers
Would pull the chairs for me to sit,
And give me their arm to cross the land.

When he took me there I walked slow
As a wolf cautious in a house,
From room to room, looking
At the hair brush on the gilded table,
At blue crystal bottles and curtains on windows,
The clothing hanging.

What different worlds.
My father's cabin was chinked with mud
And crushed shells from the sea
While they had tall buildings with stones, with water
Brought inside through golden faucets.
And outside were fountains and roads of stones.

Then I saw the bed where we,
Husband and wife, would sleep,
Surrounded by cloth.
I had never touched anything like those velvets and silks.
I touched one and I asked him,
Where did these come from?
He said men traveled the world in search of worms
That live in small rooms and eat only mulberry leaves
In order to create this silken splendor
And that I should say, "From where do these come?"
Never then did I think
One day I would feel
So much like one of those worms, like a spider
Closed into a small room.

All I knew about spiders and their strands of silk
Was their shining threads
And how they let themselves down through the world.
All I knew was that we girls used the old cobwebs to rub
against our thighs to make fishing line

And catch a trout for dinner.
I never knew anyone to weave a robe such as those my
husband gave to me or how they make soft cloth
To sleep on at night.

I went to them.
Not yet a human being in our world
And helpless against their laws.
I, who thought bringing home a trout
The greatest joy and spiders most beautiful,
Was soon caught in the web of what I did not know.
Soon told to speak only their language,
To dress in their clothing, to step into their church
And try to believe.

But on my wedding day
I wore the white gown of those worms and leaves,
A gown of closed rooms, on my wedding day.
Some said, How beautiful she is in white silk.
Others said, How could he take such a wife?
Yet they were the ones
Who later came to me in the early hours of morning
To heal their wounds,
Asking for secrecy,
Or to give them the leaves to make them fertile
Or, bleeding, to fix their doctor's shoddy work.

At first they needed me,
Woman of plants and knowledge they no longer had,
And then as I said, I was the midwife for their women

I was called upon to sign papers.
In the beginning I was part of their society.
I could speak with others and help them
Make their way in our world, and I signed in favor
Of my own people more often than not.
I went between the worlds
To settle things.
I translated the words
And I interpreted all the wild things.

I was in between.
I was, I am, the continental divide.
I am the collision of continents
Contained in the silence of a body.

I had word from my father
That they cut our trees in spite of the legal papers.
Legally they now belonged to my husband.
We hadn't thought that word in marriage, "legal,"
Or what it meant, his ownership of all of mine.
My father, how he looked I will never forget.

It is so hard to say all this
And all because of a twelve-year old heart.
I would never have dreamed
There would be no more room in our world
For birds and owls, for wolves or the elk with antlers.

They were game animals.
They were like me, the wilderness
That could be done away with.

Game.
That's what they call the hunted animals.
I used to think about that word
And all it meant. Game.
It's like the word,
Take.
Which means to kill.
And there was falconry,
Where the bird, blind with covered eyes,
Like me with no choice but to trust
My husband's arm,
The hungry bird would be unhooded
To see the world, crying out
To fly for its master.

At the same time I was spokeperson
For the slaves, my own people who labored for them.
Some of their games I learned.

Chess. With the king, queen, pawn.
They are about the life of the rich and powerful.
They are about the theft of the people
As acts of civilization. Chess. The new one: Monopoly.
All tiresome. All *take*.

My stomach grew in all this time
While he spent many hours pondering
The possibilities of the Queen.
I already had learned these possibilities in case
One day I would have to make my own moves
And take the king.

But they would never need the likes of me
to harm them.
They cleared their own trees for cattle
and now the land began to dry up and burn
In the drought they created.
They poisoned the grasses
And now the water became full of poison
Before it started to disappear.
Even the heat increased.
Then they cut the cedar trees nature sent
To cool their land, to darken it for shade.
They cursed themselves.

They didn't need a woman like me to harm them.
Later they feared some one of us, darker,

Stronger, wiser,
Would rule their ruined land where
They mined the tops of mountains.
They had no need to fear me
With my small knowledge and songs.
But oh my heart. I was killed by what they'd done
To this world I love,
The land, and all the small animals.
Oh, You small people
Of this large world.

I was only a part of their game, an animal, a pawn.
When I learned what their game was,
I was a young leader's wife, queen of dark hearts,
The aftershock of their history.

I had to remain silent
Though I grieved they cut the trees on the mountains.
I cried when the beautiful land became a world for cattle
And floating dead trees. Cattle. Chattel.
That's what they had become.
And all the living animals became units or pounds.
It was a world no longer alive.

Now men pay money to kill the fenced buffalo
as if there is pleasure in it.
They call it hunting.

History is a short thing.

My grandmother was one of those who found the women
With babies wrapped against them.
They called those times The Indian Wars.
We call them The American Wars.

At the end I said, I know what your people have done.

Now I sit imprisoned on the very land
That once belonged to my grandfather,
The world a bruise on my heart.

Black Hawk once said,
If a prophet had told us this was to happen,
None of us would ever have believed it.

Clare, I forgot the time.
I hear the keys
And you probably only want to know if I killed my own
Children, then I tell you the long story of the games,
Of how I moved from queen to pawn.
Your ears become sensitive in here.

You probably don't even hear the keys
Walking toward us.
Here, the sound of keys is everything.
Keys have meaning.
They open and close a day or night, a hope, a life.

Water

Clare, do you have children?
Two boys. How fortunate. Yes, I know this
Is not about your life.
Or do you fear me?
I wonder what you would do to save them
From being savages, as they called it, public specimens.
Or judged as mingled seed, as Leviticus said.

Yes, as for my children, they were his gold
In the surround of force.
Where I had a cup of pain,
They had the birthright, they were the gold.
In our world, we had no word for gold.
We only had yellow and more yellow.
In our green, rich valley we had a word for green
and the same word for blue. Okchamahli.
Because we were river people, river and sky,
And knew the colors where one water entered another,
Where sky met earth.

I kept my own ways
And my husband accepted with love
Or I would have been undone
By the others, taken apart
As they tried to teach me what they knew.

21

It was so little compared to what we knew,
This land and all its ways.
I, just a girl, could read the water
And when and how to travel upon it.

In all this time my stomach grew
And when it was time for my son to enter this world,
I went to the river on my horse,
The one I called My Sister.
And when I walked down the bank
And through the reeds
I walked out into the place where warm water rises
From beneath the world
And among the flowing water, the plants,
My water joined the other.
I cried out only a little
And my handsome son came swimming
To the surface of the river
As if still in the waters of my body.
He was dark like me but with a hint of golden hair.
He smiled as he came up to air.
Even before I fed him my breast,
My heart quickened with love.
I wrapped him in cloth and held him close
There at the water, his heritage.
When I returned, my husband's mother said,
What an uncivilized birth. In water, too.
And how can you wrap this infant in plain cloth?

They took him from me and wrapped him in shining cloth
And hired a nurse, one of my own people, to be with him.
I remained as much as possible,
Together, the three of us laughing and talking
With each other and the child.
At that time my man was gentle at night,
Looking at our son.
Or sometimes we walked under the trees they planted
Where the great, large old ones used to be.
He caressed my face
And he looked at the baby so softly.
I turned my heart even more toward him.

When my daughter was born
She too was smiling, the girl
Who had eyes of blue.
Coming up, no matter what they thought,
From the same waters into this world smiling,
Not shocked by a sudden life in air
Or hit into breathing.

I was young
But I knew how to bring a child to the world,
Though to them I was an animal,
As they said, Crude and barbaric,
But I never met an animal as barbaric
As a human so civilized as they.

For a time life was good.
Each morning when the sun came up
I offered pollen and tobacco
And I sang and said my prayers.
Owls cried at night,
Songbirds by day.

One evening I received a letter that my father was ill.
I wanted to go to him.
We were having a dinner
And he, the man of gold I married, said,
But we have guests.
Your job is to stay beside me.

I knew they would not miss me
After their drinks,
So I set out with Sister, my mare,
And both children.
We could ride long distances
And I crossed the water with the mare.

As we journeyed I thought
How often I had seen my husband's character
changed lately
And everything inside his skin was broken.
Corrupt is the word you would use for it now.
But then, he was a politician married to enrich
His empire before I knew it.

And it seemed we became like two magnets
That placed together fling apart.
He had already begun to stay away,
Sometimes for nights he couldn't explain
Except by lies.

I went to my father.
My father didn't even notice I was there at first.
He was crying and talking about the last time
He saw his brother
When they took him away to school.
I didn't want this to be what my father saw
The day before he left this world.
And so I showed him the grandchildren and he Named them
Eho and Nakni
And then he was gone
As if his work was done.

I remained for three days
In our different world,
My homeland of beauty.

We have a story
For every place on the land,
A world remembered, loved, revered.

I thought how my destiny was to be a bridge
And that then one day it would break

To stop the others from crossing
Over the broken treaties.

On the day I returned
I saw my husband standing with a woman
Who had long hair down her back,
Hair yellow as the first flowers of spring.
She saw my daughter. I heard her say,
Isn't she charming for being one of them?
I cast a cold eye on them both
And rode the mare, My Sister, right up to them.
They knew they'd been seen.
My son held his arms down to his father.
I lifted him and my husband,
I still call him that, the man of stone
Did not take him at first
Until I told him. There was nothing more to him.
Then I took the children
And rode away with them.

It has been many years.
I saw my husband kiss the new woman
And still it hurts.

I thought, he loved this young woman
more than he loved me.
I felt pain in one chamber of my heart.
He was like a child,
He always wanted more.
Her father had the more.
And would give him a place in the world he wanted,
The politician, the man who never had to grow food
Or work for any other man.

It happened so quickly
That I was locked out of my life,
My world, my bed.
He sent a messenger
To say I was to go into exile.
At first I took the children to the woods.
The servants, my own people, brought us food
But there was a chill in the air, in everything.
We went to my childhood friends
And lived for a time
In the servant's quarter.
I hid my weeping while the children played together,
Hidden.

She was a thief, that young woman.
She slept in my bed.
She slept with my husband.
And right away, to secure her life

She was pregnant with her own child
While we were in exile in our own land.

Her father, something of a King, sent a message
Saying it will be a good marriage of gold and money,
A good position in the world
For your children and you will be cared for.
He didn't even know my name
Or that now my life counted for nothing in this world.

Rejoice, he said.
Your son may be a king one day.
My marriage became illegal under new rules.
My husband, a man nothing could touch,
Not even our memories,
Married a woman who saw my children
As playthings,
As souvenirs of a people gone,
A people noble and savage at the same time.
When did he last hold one of them?
When did he last speak?
He'd always said
They were such trouble.

You know there is no love deeper
Than mother and child.
He was already taking away my life.

And then one day they came on horseback
And as I had foreseen, they took my children
Even as I fought them
And with my own horse, I chased after them
Through the splashing water,
But they turned on me, to kill me.

She was large with child when I returned
And I hid behind the trees and underbrush
Like an animal to watch.
She dressed my daughter in a golden gown
And placed a crown of flowers on her head.
I stepped out. What are you doing? I asked.
You never dressed her well, she said.
I took the crown of flowers away.
Mother, they smell so sweet, my daughter said.
I took them off her dark hair.
Eho, I said, Let's go.
My daughter wanted her flowers back.
How little did she know.
It isn't good for us here, I said.
We have to leave the flowers behind
And we will get more.

You Indian! She said to me. You savage.
I want my flowers back.
My child said that.

She hated what I was,
Without knowing she was the same.
And there was hate in her eyes.
Oh my heart.

They had taken her from me
In so many ways.
But not my son. He stood strong.
He said, Mother I will come to you.

I had the power only to weep.

Chambers

How are your children?
I think of how it must be
When you look at them in your arms,
Asleep with soft lashes
Against their skin,
and hair that smells so sweet.

You think how first the body makes room for them.
Then the heart makes room.
We open and close
Like tides.
The heart is the motion of water.

I brought this gift for you.
It's a chambered nautilus.
It belonged to my father.
I've kept it all this time.
Do you know it forms its chambers
By the cycles of the moon?
When these animals are alive,
They rise to the surface of water each night.
And they descend back into the depths by day.

It has many chambers,
Unlike the human heart,
Said to have only four.
Mine had six,
All of them broken.
Still, I remember children asleep in my arms.
My heart had so much room for their sweetness.

When they were born, my children became curiosities.
I used to sit in my chamber
And think of Black Elk, the healing man with a great vision,
And Sitting Bull, the great and tender warrior
Who cared so for his people,
Who had no choice but to be in Buffalo Bill's Circus.
We were what they were, a spectacle.
I was wise enough to know
We were objects from the other world for them to behold.
This broke another chamber of my heart.

At least the servants were my child-mates,
My own people who did not envy me.
They understood our position
And were kind to me. They came to me in secret
And with happiness we recalled our childhoods.

Then one day another chamber of my heart broke.
My own son said, "Don't you know what you are?"
And went to his room in his father's mansion,

Leaving me darker, older, alone.
And there were many rooms in his father's mansion.
The children were given presents to stay there.
Now I sit in my prison chamber and hear the stories.
The women tell their stories, all but the one who never takes
Off her Sunglasses, and we will never know
Any secret places in her heart or soul.

One day I watched the queen of the world
Hit my son.
Another chamber of my heart broke.
I moved from tree to tree, watching,
As if I had no choice but to hide in my own land.
And my daughter had a look on her face
As if she'd become one of them.
She wore a dress of new red cloth and bangles and charms.
She held a blonde doll and she was happy.
It broke my heart.
They were children he never loved,
Now such curiosities
To the new wife—and I was in exile.
I heard the princess say of my daughter,
Is she not cute as a little doll?
In my life I slipped from queen to pawn.
There was no more belonging,
I was the bear who wandered out of her den to find
The land changed,

The wolf mother trying to protect her small ones
As they were being smoked out.

Recently I wept so hard
They took me to the little house
That they call "isolation chamber."
They don't know I like it in there.
I like the silence.
The way I hear my own heart beat
And remember I am alive.
The way I can dream of the green world I came from
The waters flowing,
The ocean nights when the shining nautilus
Came to the surface.

Sometimes it is hard to dream when women are crying.
It is hard to breathe in any chamber where nothing is green.
They know I long to be outdoors in the lush
Green of the island,
Hearing the sound of waves and wind, to see
Round stones and soft mosses.
I cannot live in the darkness of these rooms.
I only dwell here
In this chambered building.

There is not a word for jail in our language.
When someone goes wrong we send them away.

34

I was the sent-away woman.
I was sent from the man
Who wanted power more than love.
I think of that word, power, and what it means.
It means you feed your people, you help the world.
I never understood what else there was to it
But I watched its struggles daily, its games.

He was a man like in their Bible.
He wrestled angels.
In the end the angels won, or maybe lost.
It all confuses me.
When he saw me watching my children,
He called my girl and took her inside to her chambers.
He held the shoulder of her dress.
He did not touch her hand or lift her.
I saw his shadow behind him, from the light.
I know what lives in shadows.
There is a shadow of every woman here, in every cell.
There is darkness in some chamber of every heart.

When I think of these things
I lose my strength
I could live better in the caves on the hillsides
Where trees are bent by the wind,
Where crystals form slowly, so slowly,
Growing with each drop of water
To meet one another one day.

Time does this to all of us in some way.
But here, it is hard being in a world with so little light
And I am one who needs to have my hands in the earth,
Planting, searching through earth and clay
And once I even loved the caves underground
Where I would find the minerals of life
But then I had the freedom to walk
In the wide circle of sunlight
In any place I wished.

Robes

Once I wore robes and stood straight as the trees.
It was said that the people of our world
were strong and generous and knew peace.
We were beautiful.
We were Indians. Indios.
In Dios. It means *In God*.
Remember, it was Columbus
Who said that when he first saw our graceful lives.
It is how I received my name.
But soon we were savages, beasts, animals.
We were tortured in ways you don't want to hear.
I am a wolf. That is my clan.
I am what they feared.
I am a woman from wild forests
And trees with the wind through green leaves.

Yet I, the barbarian,
Wore robes and stood straight as trees.
He said he brought me out of barbarism
Into society,
Out of superstition
Into civility.
I wore robes and stood straight.

But I did remove his words. They were an ugly cloth.
I took off my memories.
Now I try to undress a five hundred year old wound.

I never wanted to meet great heroes or kings,
I only wanted to love.
Yet I met them, and they tell me
I stood tall and beautiful in my robes,
Majestic.
Who would have thought I was hiding an evil heart
Inside my robes of splendor
Until they took my children.
How many women have been criminals for love?
So many I could name. They fill this place:
Sarah. Maria. Lenore.
All of us equal in here,
This house of the broken.
What I did for my husband,
I gave him all a man could desire,
He, who married me only for our land, our trees.
I helped him stake a claim to my people's world.
If I could do it over
I would never have gone away
With the thief of human hearts.

But I lived by the heart.
It was a dictator.

All I did was for him.
I gave him all a man could desire
Including gold. I betrayed for him.

Nature is full of omens, they say.
That day my husband and the new queen married
A mare broke loose and went wild.
She tore a stallion with her teeth from neck to foot.
A fish caught on fire as soon as it came from the water.
Then, strangest of all,
A lion walked through town.
The people were afraid.
Perhaps it was the uniforms of the armed ones.
They stood behind him.
They say I know magic.
It isn't true.
I didn't know the meaning of these things until late.

The cures passed down to me by the older ones
Were never magic, but wisdom and knowledge
About what plants would make old men have children again.

I never wanted to harm any soul.
I would have gone away from there
And never harmed the thief of this human heart.
It isn't comfort I search for now,
It isn't forgiveness.
It is to change time.

I can see that you think I am innocent,
That my skin was the prison
In the world of the beautiful and plenty.
Do not think that I am innocent, but know:
I did not kill my children.
I do grieve I had my children carry the golden wrap.
They should have been away from there.

But while I was banned to the desert
I considered how the king was taken in their games.
I thought, they love gold,
I will make this robe of gold.
I will make it of cloth that shines,
Cloth that came from the sun.
I gathered the plants myself and I gathered the dyes.
They were given me by the plants themselves.
I was not my father's daughter at that time,
Given to such an act.
Yet I was led to them.
I stripped the plants thin,
Careful not to touch the heart of the reed.
I wove bad intentions into her wedding shawl.

While they prepared the wedding
They sent the children to me.
My son said, See, I would be back for you.
Dear boy.

The clouds lifted that day
And the poison plants that would become her robe
Were so beautiful and gold, I knew she would place it
over her shoulders,
My wedding gift.
It was a living thing.

And when she placed it on her body,
I thought, she will look so bright.
They'll think I harbor no bad feelings.
But the children wanted to carry it.

I knew there were dark trades in the light.
Oh I don't mean the trades of the women here.
But trades like my husband made for power and money,
The lives of children, the hearts of women.
And all I wanted was my children with me.
You don't want to think
of those darker chambers
in the heart.

There was something I have no name for inside of me.
I said I was spinning the sun. I was weaving
The glint of the webs that shine in morning light.
She would love the beauty of the garment.
Part of my own wedding dress was in it.

I told the children,
Do not touch it. It will tarnish.
I closed it into a box so they could present it.
I would have taken it myself had I been allowed,
But I was not good enough to enter my own land.
My children looked proud to bear a gift
That had once been my own wedding gown,
But now it was from wild fields,
And poison.
And yet no doctor could prove a poison
Entered the skin through gold, it wore so thin in blood.
So I would prove innocent of that crime
And all except my husband would not know
What I had done.
They died from their love of gold.
The scene of their pain was so terrible,
I ran to take the children away,
Away from those who would keep them.
I thought we'd one day play the stick game
Or skip stones in the river.
But the men were fast and they caught us.
I heard them say what they were doing to the children.
No. Not the children!
I tried to break free.
I yelled, I'm the one.
I'm the one who did it.
But before my eyes, they picked up stones.

Before my eyes they threw them.
While others held me
I heard first one stone
Taking the life of a future king whose fate was now
Undone.
They feared the future that would have been
If my son became their king, mixed blood.
I will never forget the sound of stones against the body.
I would have died with them if I could.
But they killed my children and held me still
While I screamed and then fell helpless.
My little ones were placed upon my weeping body.
When he arrived, Oh house of blood.
They said to him I killed the children.
I was their wolf. They say I killed them like a wolf.
And I had walked out of my den
Covered with blood, carrying them.
I said, Look at them, my dear.
There are not cuts, no wounds,
Only the marks of the stones of these men.
He never even came to see the children
Or how they died.
He never came to see his own.
I was guilty by word alone.
Not one of us was loved.
We were minor stars,
Nameless in the dark matter of his universe.

The house of cards fell before me.

I thought I knew how their kingdoms worked
But they were shuffled and lives put back in new ways.
I only wrapped my children in beautiful robes.
I wrapped them.
And now I am the wolf mother sent away
To live behind bars. You've seen it in the zoo,
The look in our eyes,
Sleeping on corners of concrete,
Urine along the edges of the floor,
Animals. Beasts from other worlds to stare at.
I am one of those.
A game animal.
A pawn.
I am one of those not civilized.

It turns out I am their savage, after all
And all the doors have closed
on the wilderness of my heart.
Yet I remember the world,
The sounds of the water,
The stars in the dark of night,
The fresh wind.

Now I bow to all I meet
When once I stood straight and tall
And wore a robe of velvet cloth.

But I remember songs and people dancing.
Me, with my robes of skin,
My robes of fur, my robes of silk and velvet
Born from a race of people
Who came straight from this beloved earth.

In Here

I see you continue thinking I am moral.
You have compassion. It is just because
You know how much injustice exists in the world,
That my skin was the prison of their plenty, just property
All along—and how could it not have come to this.
It's true I am innocent of killing my children,
But I am not innocent
Of the death of my husband's new wife.

In here there are few windows,
Just the tiny one
The moon passes across
At times. She lays down her light on the floor
Only a moment
Before picking it up and leaving again.
They took the moon and sun away from me.
The moon changed the tides.
She changes even the rivers.

Some believe I am a political prisoner.
They stand outside the doors and call.
Others believe I killed my children.
Others know they were stoned

By those large men who feared
A mixed-blood child would come to rule.

As for me now, it doesn't matter that I am here.
I am from a world of secrets like prison doors
That never open.

I was the aftershock of history and colliding lands.
This is what happens to those like me.

I have white hair now,
White as the Milky Way at night,
The path souls travel, we call it.
White as the moon that visits now and then,
Or snow in the north I visited
So many years ago
As we traveled about, myself so in love
And I still feel the pain of an ordinary lover.
Worse, the pain a mother feels when she loses children
Is something that never stops beating the heart.
One man in another land said they could hear me crying
Far away. They came to ask if I would go away with them
Where I'd be safe. Safe from what, I asked,
So innocent then.

I felt only what American Horse said.
He said, I feel a wish to go out in the forest
And cover my head with a blanket
So that I can see no more
And have a chance to think over what I've seen.

Now at times I fold clothing in the laundry.
Savage me.
I fold it flat and creased and perfect.
And at night I cover my head
And think of what I've seen.

In here women cry in the night.
They talk in their sleep,
The forgotten ones
Falling as if there is no bottom to their fall.

In our stories, the world grew from songs and love.
Now I wake to find tears falling from my eyes.
How I want to go to a high place in the mountains
Or to the water that is in my blood.
I want to go to the beautiful world
Where we loved even the spiders.

We had horses and knew where the wild birds nested.
I want just once to see where our corn grew,
In the footprints of our ancestors.
They taught us about souls and prophets.
As for us, we had no word for soul
Because the whole earth is our soul.
We are children of water and light, earth and wind.
As for water, did I tell you I knew how to read it,
When to travel, how to move the canoe,
How to turn into the quiet places of trees in water
And silence deep in the soul.

Some nights I look through the wall
Out to where I know there is an ocean,
Thinking of sea turtles and flying fish in silver waters.
The Europeans did not know navigation.
They had to take homing birds
With them on ocean voyages
To find their way home,
While we traveled by the stars.

We are children of the sun, as well.
It was another of our ancestors.
Now I am chlorophyll
And so I also work in the spring garden.
I place the seeds and sing with them.
I change the light to something green with my hands.

I change the dark of earth to light of sky,
My hands in the earth, grateful hands
In their own world.

Here at night someone is always crying.
I think I told you that.
Sometimes from the geography of my aging heart,
I go to that person
By day and offer something to them,
A piece of chocolate that came from a package sealed
And not taken by any guards.
Sometimes, I give them earrings I have made.

Listen, do you hear those wings? A bird is here.
A night hawk. No, not a bird.
What am I thinking?
It is the woman who always shuffles cards.
She shuffles and lays them out,
Then shuffles again.
She used to be a gambler.
She always won. She always won at cards
While I saw houses of them fall.

Other Selected Works by Linda Hogan

Poetry

Seeing Through the Sun (1985)
Savings (1988)
The Book of Medicines (1993)
Rounding the Human Corners (2008)

Fiction

Mean Spirit (1991)
Solar Storms (1997)
Power (1999)
People of the Whale (2008)

Essays

Dwellings: A Spiritual History of the Living World (2007)
Inner Journey: Views from Native Traditions (2009)

Memoir

The Woman Who Watches Over the World (2002)

Nonfiction

Sightings: The Gray Whales' Mysterious Journey
(with Brenda Peterson, 2003)

About the Author

Linda Hogan was inducted into the Chickasaw Nation Hall of Fame in 2007, and currently is Writer-in-Residence for the Chickasaw Nation. An internationally recognized public speaker and writer of poetry, fiction, and essays, she is the recipient of a National Endowment for the Arts Fellowship, a Guggenheim Fellowship and the Lifetime Achievement Award from the Native Writers Circle of the Americas, among numerous other honors.

Hogan is the author of five collections of poetry, her most recent being *Rounding the Human Corners* (2008), which was nominated for the Pulitzer Prize. *The Book of Medicines* (1993) was a finalist for the National Book Critics Circle Award. Other poetry collections have received the Colorado Book Award, Minnesota State Arts Board Grant, an American Book Award, and a prestigious Lannan Fellowship from the Lannan Foundation.

People of the Whale (2008) is Hogan's most recent novel. Other notable novels include *Mean Spirit,* (1991), winner of the Oklahoma Book Award, the Mountains and Plains Book Award, and a finalist for the Pulitzer Prize, *Solar Storms* (1997), a finalist for the International IMPAC Dublin Literary Award in Ireland, and *Power*, also a finalist for the International IMPAC.

Her nonfiction includes *Dwellings: A Spiritual History of the Living World* (2007) and *The Woman Who Watches Over the World: A Native Memoir* (2002). With Brenda Peterson, she wrote *Sightings: The Gray Whales' Mysterious Journey* (2003) for National Geographic Books. Hogan has also edited several anthologies on nature and spirituality, including *Inner Journey: Views from Native Traditions* (2009). Hogan's script, *Everything Has a Spirit,* was a PBS documentary on American Indian Religious Freedom. She recently completed a short documentary for the REEL/NATIVE series, *A Feel for the Land* (PBS/American Experience).

She has also worked with Native youth in horse programs and continues to teach Creative Writing. A former Professor at the University of Colorado, she was only the second minority woman to become a Full Professor there. She now lives and works in Oklahoma, where she continues to teach creative writing. Hogan has been involved for 15 years with the

Native Science Dialogues and the new Native American Academy, and for many years with the SEED Graduate Institute in Albuquerque. She is a faculty member for the Indigenous Education Institute and a fellow of the Black Earth Institute.

Hogan was one of two invited writer-speakers at the United Nations Forum in 2008. Her work has been translated into most major languages by the U.S. Information Office, and she speaks and reads from her work both nationally and internationally. She was a Plenary Speaker at the Environmental Literature Conference in Turkey in November 2009, and presented a 90 minute program at the International Congress of the Parliament of World Religions in Melbourne in 2009.

Acknowledgments

I would like to acknowledge first my support system of friends. We've discussed this project over the years. They include Marilyn Auer, Kathleen Cain, Amethyst First Rider, LeAnne Howe, Allison Hedge-Coke, Cherríe Moraga, Deborah Miranda, Lisa Wagner, Julia Weber Walker, Frieda Clark, Laura Clark, my cousins Becky Travis and Doris McAtee, and those equally important whose names escape me at this last moment. Forgive me if I have forgotten you.

I am especially grateful to David Curtis for his ever faithful support for this work and for listening to it all, even when it frightened him! James Wallace, who wanted to produce it first, does not go without thanks.

I want to acknowledge the support of The Chickasaw Nation and our visionary leaders, Bill Anoatubby and Jefferson Keel, who have offered me the freedom to travel and write, to do research on our tribal matters, history, and archaeology. Lona Barrick I thank for now offering a first performance or reading of this work.

But this work is the story of my own world and time, that of many other indigenous women, so I thank and send beauty to all your lives wherever you may be. We always seem to know and care for one another whether we exist in the Saami world, in Maori life, or in our own Southeastern tribal nations.

Special gratitude goes to Simon Ortiz for introductory materials and to Lois Beardslee for her Foreword, as well. Also, to Pam Uschuk for sending me to Bryce Milligan, editor and publisher of Wings Press, who has offered significant information and advice. Special thanks for his belief in this manuscript.

And for Euripides, who told what was imagined but confessed what was real.

Chumashki. Thank you all.

Works Consulted

Though this account of Indios is fictionalized, it is based on the story of Medea. Medea's aunt was said by some to be Circe, her father a sorcerer, her Grandfather Helios, the Sun God.

This poem and performance piece is based loosely on Medea, who fell in love with Jason and promised to help him; but she was always only a "barbarian" to him. While *Indios* is set in contemporary times, it is based on the stories said to be honest and true about the Corinthians killing Medea's children, not the mother herself.

I have used many sources, including Euripides, who said that the children of Medea were murdered by the Corinthians, who then had a plague come over them. In the original myth, the children were murdered by the Corinthians.

Some of the other sources are, to the best of my knowledge-keeping:

Medea: Essays on Medea in Myth, Literature, Philosophy and Art, by Sarah Lies Johnston, Princeton University Press.

Medea: Essays on Medea in Myth, Literature, Philosophy, and Art, edited by James Joseph Claus and Sarah Iles Johnston (Princeton University Press, 1997).

Related Scholia to Euripide's Medea, Denys Lionel Page, ed., Oxford 1938 (1967).

Greek Mythology website (http://www.maicar. com/GML/), 1997, by Carolos Parada and Maicer Fortag.

Some ancient commentaries suggest that Creon's relatives killed the children and spread the story that Medea had murdered them. Other readings say they were stoned to death by the Corinthians, or bled to death at the hands of the Corinthian women. I am assuming the first position in my writing of the contemporary story. It seems right.

Wings Press was founded in 1975 by Joanie Whitebird and Joseph F. Lomax, both deceased, as "an informal association of artists and cultural mythologists dedicated to the preservation of the literature of the nation of Texas." Publisher, editor and designer since 1995, Bryce Milligan is honored to carry on and expand that mission to include the finest in American writing—meaning all of the Americas, without commercial considerations clouding the choice to publish or not to publish. Technically a "for profit" press, Wings receives only occasional underwriting from individuals and institutions who wish to support our vision. For this we are very grateful.

Wings Press attempts to produce multicultural books, chapbooks, ebooks, CDs, DVDs and broadsides that, we hope, enlighten the human spirit and enliven the mind. Everyone ever associated with Wings has been or is a writer, and we know well that writing is a trans- formational art form capable of changing the world, primarily by allowing us to glimpse something of each other's souls. Good writing is innovative, insightful, and interesting. But most of all it is honest.

Likewise, Wings Press is committed to treating the planet itself as a partner. Thus the press uses as much recycled material as possible, from the paper on which the books are printed to the boxes in which they are shipped.

As Robert Dana wrote in *Against the Grain,* "Small press publishing is personal publishing. In essence, it's a matter of personal vision, personal taste and courage, and personal friendships." Welcome to our world.

Colophon

This first edition of *Indios*, by Linda
Hogan, has been printed on 55 pound EB
natural paper containing a high percent-
age of recycled fiber. Titles have been set
in Parisian type, the text in Papyrus type.
All Wings Press books are designed and
produced by Bryce Milligan.

On-line catalogue and ordering
available at
www.wingspress.com

Wings Press titles are distributed
to the trade by the
Independent Publishers Group
www.ipgbook.com
and in Europe by
www.gazellebookservices.co.uk

Also available as an ebook.